MYSTERIOUS WIMBLEDON

BY

RUTH MURPHY AND CLIVE WHICHELOW

ILLUSTRATIONS

BY

BRIAN GOLDSMITH

Published by

Enigma Publishing
51 Cecil Road
Wimbledon
SW19 1JR

First edition October 1994

ISBN 0 9524297 0 5

Printed by Roebuck Press

CONTENTS

INTRODUCTION

Much has been written about the history of Wimbledon but there is another side to it that is less well known. Underneath the peaceful exterior lie a number of strange tales.

You probably know that the Lawn Tennis Championships are held at the All England Club in Church Road, but did you know that one of the competitors was once convicted of murder? Or that Henry VIII came close to death in Wimbledon? Or that Wimbledon Theatre boasts not one but two ghosts?

Hillside was once the home of a spiritualist group and a number of residents have experienced poltergeist activity and strange occurrences in their homes. Could there be a connection?

Names of well known people emerge. Marconi, inventor of the wireless telegraph; William Stead - the psychic and author; the wife of the vicar of Borley Rectory (once claimed to be the most haunted house in England). What are the strange stories that connect these people with Wimbledon?

Duels on the common, allegations of witchcraft, the wrath of God unleashed in the Mirabilis Annus. It's a long way from lawn tennis and Wombles but a very interesting side of Wimbledon that you may not know about.

'Mysterious Wimbledon' attempts to uncover some of these strange stories and unusual events, as well as to debunk some of the myths and misconceptions associated with the area.

The Centre Court Murderer

THE CENTRE COURT MURDERER

Wimbledon champion convicted of murder! Unbelievable but true.

In 1879 a 25 year old tennis player called Vere Thomas St. Leger Goold won the men's singles title in Dublin. Following this success he was soon playing at the Wimbledon championships where he was runner-up in the men's finals.

St. Leger Goold's career met with a modest amount of success, tapering off, until 1883, when he suddenly disappeared from the tennis circuit. Nothing strange about that, you may think.

But in August 1907, a trunk and a bag were deposited in the cloakroom at Marseilles station in France. A strange smell emanated from the luggage, and the porter, whose suspicions were aroused, contacted the police.

When the dismembered corpse of a woman was found inside the trunk, the couple who had deposited the luggage were arrested.

The man who had left the luggage was none other than Vere Thomas St. Leger Goold and the woman with him his wife. The remains in the trunk were that of a woman who St. Leger Goold claimed had approached him and his wife for a loan. He claimed that while she was with them her lover had burst into the room and killed her. The couple panicked and decided to get rid of the body themselves.

The dead woman was Mme. Emma Liven who had in fact visited the Goolds to reclaim a loan. It appeared that the couple frequently gambled and regularly drank and quarrelled. Their standard of living had deteriorated and they began to borrow and then to steal. The culmination of their lifestyle led them to murder.

St. Leger Goold was sentenced to penal servitude for life and his wife received the death penalty. This was later commuted to a life sentence on appeal.

St. Leger Goold died on Devil's Island on 8th September 1909 and Mrs. Goold died in prison in 1914.

The full story of St. Leger Goold, by Alan Little can be found in the Wimbledon Tennis Museum at the All England Club in Church Road.

THE MOST HAUNTED HOUSE IN ENGLAND AND THE WIMBLEDON CONNECTION

The connection between Wimbledon and Borley Rectory in Essex is a fascinating one. In the 1930s Borley Rectory was known as the 'most haunted house in England'. It was brought to the attention of the public by a number of articles which appeared in the Daily Mirror in June 1929 with headings such as 'Ghost visits to a Rectory' and 'Tales of headless coachman and lonely nun.'

What is less well known is that one of the key players in the Borley saga, Marianne Foyster, wife of the Reverend Lionel Algernon Foyster led a life of duplicity and deceit.

The Foysters moved into the Rectory in October 1930 and poltergeist activity heightened whilst they were in residence. The story seems to have gained credence due to the fact that the events were reported by a clergyman and his wife.

Their case was investigated by Harry Price, the well known 'psychist' of the day, who even went so far as to suggest that Marianne Foyster was responsible for much of the so called poltergeist activity. He wrote a number of books about Borley.

During the Foysters' stay at Borley they rented the Rectory cottage to a Francois d'Arles, and Marianne soon began a sexual relationship with him.

In February 1933, d'Arles and Marianne opened a florists shop in Worple Road in Wimbledon called 'Jonquille et Cie' (which is now the site of the Sainsbury's supermarket). They befriended a family also living in Worple Road who assumed that Marianne and d'Arles were married. Marianne lived this double life until 1934, spending weekdays in Wimbledon and returning to Borley at weekends. Her husband seemed to have no objection to this strange arrangement. The florist business foundered in 1934 and Marianne left Wimbledon. She split with d'Arles who subsequently tried to blackmail her.

The Foysters left Borley Rectory after 15 months occupancy. In February 1935 she married bigamously and lived with her new husband and Lionel Algernon Foyster (telling her new husband that he was her father).

Lionel Algernon Foyster died in 1945. A relative believed that Marianne had poisoned him. Marianne fled to the USA in 1945 and married again, leaving her children behind. She was still living there in the 1980s.

THE MYSTERIOUS DEATH OF 'IRISH ROSE' ATKINS

In the early hours of the morning of July 14th 1938 a woman's body was found by a motorist in Somerset Road near the All England Tennis Club.

At first he thought she had been the victim of a hit and run incident but on closer inspection found that she had been battered about the face and head and had been stabbed. There were also tyre marks across her body.

Police enquiries soon established that the body was that of 'Irish Rose' Atkins, a prostitute who had frequented the area around Inner Park Road for the past three years. On the night of July 13th Rose had been seen talking to a man in a green van and then driving off with him.

The van was later found by police smeared with the blood of Rose Atkins and containing her handbag and a leather knife covered in blood.

The driver of the van, George Brain, had disappeared shortly after the body had been found and had told a friend that he was intending to get a boat to Spain. He had been working as a van driver for a firm of boot repairers at St Pancras and left owing them £32 in takings collected from customers.

Police were unable to locate Brain until he was spotted by farm labourers ten days later on the Isle of Sheppey. He had been sleeping rough on the cliffs at Sheerness since his disappearance and was said to be 'ravenously hungry' when arrested.

At his trial it was found that Brain had been asked for money by Rose Atkins who had said she was in financial difficulties. When Brain refused she threatened to inform his employers that he had been using the firm's van that evening. Brain hit her with a starting handle and maintained that then 'everything went blank'.

Rose had been badly beaten and dumped out of the van, which was then reversed over her. Although Brain maintained that he could not remember killing her he was found guilty and sentenced to death.

He was hanged at Wandsworth prison on November 1st 1938.

```
*  *  *  *  *  *  *  *  *  *  *  *  *  *  *  *  *  *  *  *  *  *  *  *  *  *  *  *    *
*                                                                                   *
*    Neither Caesar's Camp nor Caesar's Well has any connection   *
*    with Caesar at all.  The names appear to have been bestowed  *
*    by a Nineteenth Century mapmaker for reasons known only to   *
*    himself.  The Camp is believed to date from around 600-800   *
*    BC.                                                            *
*                                                                   *
*  *  *  *  *  *  *  *  *  *  *  *  *  *  *  *  *  *  *  *  *  *  *  *  *  *  *  *  *    *
```

A WITCH IN WIMBLEDON

In 1569 Jane Baldwyn of Wimbledon was accused of witchcraft. Over a period of three years she was said to have bewitched and killed three of the villagers and four pigs.

Her husband, John, was one of the chief farmers in Wimbledon and the fourth wealthiest resident. He was highly respected and the accusations against his wife would therefore have come as a great shock.

In 1566 a local girl, Elizabeth Bonham died though at the time not much notice was taken of her death. Then in 1567 Richard Hollingsworth, a one year old child died and Jane Baldwyn was accused by two gentlemen, one the boy's father, stating that she had 'bewitched' the infant.

Jane declared her innocence and again nothing was done. In March 1569, a man called William Walter lost four pigs and insisted that Jane had 'bewitched' them.

It was a month later that things came to a tragic conclusion. On April 12th 1569, Helen Lingard died, two months after the birth of her thirteenth child. Helen was the wife of the local miller, Hugh Lingard, who accused Jane of the crime. She was arrested and tried. Although she pleaded not guilty to the charge against her relating to Elizabeth Bonham and Walter's pigs, for some unknown reason she agreed that she was responsible for the deaths of Richard Hollingsworth and Helen Lingard.

She was found guilty and sentenced to hang. This sentence was commuted to a years' imprisonment and an order to stand in the pillory on a number of consecutive days.

John Baldwyn died in 1583. Jane was not mentioned again and it is not known what happened to the unfortunate woman.

A Witch in Wimbledon

GHOST ON THE LINE

Have you ever heard of a machine that could contact the dead? Guglielmo Marconi, inventor of the wireless radio strongly believed that this was possible.

Gothic Lodge, just off Southside was once the home of Sir William Preece and Marconi was a frequent visitor. Sir William was Chief Engineer at the Post Office and Marconi once sent messages to the Post Office in London via a transmitter set up in the garden of Gothic Lodge.

Marconi believed that an invisible electrical energy permeated the universe and that this carried an imprint of the whole of life and world events.

He attempted to build a machine that was delicate enough to capture these impressions and able to contact other planes of existence.

He was not worried about controversy. After all, scientists had stated that it was not possible to send short wave wireless messages around the globe and he had proved them wrong.

Sadly, Marconi died in 1937 before the machine he had attempted to build was complete, but it was not the end of research into the subject.

Today, EVP, or Electronic Voice Phenomenon (voices of the departed picked up on tape recorders, telephones and other electrical equipment) is still being investigated on both sides of the Atlantic.

```
* * * * * * * * * * * * * * * * * * * * * * * * * * * *  *
*                                                         *
*    An underground tunnel was built between the Duchess  *
*    of Marlborough's house and the nearby servants'      *
*    quarters so that the view above ground would not be  *
*    spoiled by the sight of the servants scurrying backwards *
*    and forwards. The tunnel is still in existence today and *
*    runs under the playing fields of Ricards Lodge High  *
*    School in Lake Road.                                 *
*                                                         *
* * * * * * * * * * * * * * * * * * * * * * * * * * * *  *
```

A VICTORIAN MURDER

George Henry Lamson, a doctor, finally succeeded in murdering his nephew Percy John on 3rd December 1881.

Lamson had got into financial difficulty due to his addiction to morphine. He resorted to lying and cheating to appear successful to others but by 1881 he was in desperate need of new finance.

He had a nephew, Percy who adored him. Unfortunately Percy was crippled with a curvature of the spine and paralysis of the lower limbs. If Percy were to die, Lamson knew that his wife would inherit the then princely sum of £700.

In 1878 when Percy was 15, Lamson invited him to spend the summer holidays with him on the Isle of Wight. During this holiday Lamson unsuccessfully tried to poison him. Percy suffered from severe vomiting but survived.

Lamson's financial situation worsened and in 1881 he decided to try again. He arranged to visit Percy at the school he attended in Wimbledon, Blenheim Special School in St Georges Road.

He visited the school on the 3rd of December. When he arrived he was offered a glass of sherry by the Headmaster, Mr. Bedbrook. Lamson asked if he could have some sugar with his sherry, an odd request, but one that was granted. A bowl of caster sugar was brought to him.

Lamson then produced three slices of Dundee cake from his bag and passed a slice to Percy and a slice to Mr. Bedbrook. He also brought from his bag some empty capsules into which he poured some of the caster sugar. He then asked Percy to show Mr. Bedbrook how easy it was to swallow one of these. Percy obliged. Soon after this Lamson left hurriedly saying that he had to catch a train, commenting to Bedbrook on the way out that he thought Percy looked very ill.

Later that evening Percy was vomiting and seriously ill. He died later on that night after falling into a coma.

The cause of death could not be established immediately but an autopsy revealed a raisin in Percy's stomach containing aconitine, a deadly poison extracted from the Monkshood plant.

When Lamson's name was mentioned at the inquest a pharmacist from the city of London recognised it and remembered Lamson purchasing aconitine.

Lamson's trial opened at the Old Bailey on 8th March 1882 and a guilty verdict was returned. Lamson eventually admitted the crime and was hanged at Wandsworth prison on April 18th 1882.

KIDNAP IN ARTHUR ROAD

In December 1969 Mrs. Muriel McKay was abducted from her home in Arthur Road.

Two brothers, Arthur and Nizamodcen Hosein mistakenly thought that Mrs. McKay was the wife of the News of the World proprietor Rupert Murdoch. She was in fact the wife of Alex McKay the acting chairman .

Mr McKay had returned home on Monday 29th of December 1969 to find his wife missing and the house in a state of disarray. The front door was open, furniture overturned, and drawers ransacked.

Shortly after this, a man claiming to represent the Mafia telephoned with a ransom demand for £1million. In the meantime police searched the ponds in Wimbledon Park and on Wimbledon Common but without success.

Repeated failed attempts were made to collect the ransom money and the Hosein brothers were eventually arrested. Rooks Farm in Essex, (which Arthur Hosein owned) was searched but the police found nothing.

The brothers were taken to the magistrates court in Queens Road Wimbledon on February 11th and after numerous delays the case went to the Old Bailey on June 16th.

They still protested their innocence but were eventually found guilty and both were jailed for life for the murder.

It is believed that Muriel McKay was murdered at Rooks Farm and there were stories in the tabloid press that her body had been fed to pigs.

Whatever the truth of the matter, Muriel McKay was never seen again.

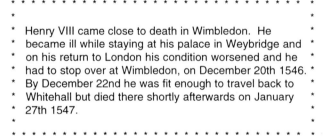

```
*  *  *  *  *  *  *  *  *  *  *  *  *  *  *  *  *  *  *  *  *  *  *  *  *  *
*                                                                        *
*   Henry VIII came close to death in Wimbledon.  He                     *
*   became ill while staying at his palace in Weybridge and              *
*   on his return to London his condition worsened and he                *
*   had to stop over at Wimbledon, on December 20th 1546.                *
*   By December 22nd he was fit enough to travel back to                 *
*   Whitehall but died there shortly afterwards on January               *
*   27th 1547.                                                           *
*                                                                        *
*  *  *  *  *  *  *  *  *  *  *  *  *  *  *  *  *  *  *  *  *  *  *  *  *  *
```

WILLIAM THOMAS STEAD - COMMUNICATION WITH THE DEPARTED

Not only did William Thomas Stead believe in life after death, he found that the dead could communicate through him.

He lived in Cambridge House in Wimbledon and had a very successful career as a journalist and writer. Over the years his interest in the supernatural increased.

In 1891 Stead collected a number of ghost stories and published them. The first volume was called "Real Ghost Stories" and the second "More Ghost Stories".

In 1890 a young American journalist, Julia Ames had visited Stead at his home in Wimbledon. Soon after this she returned to Boston where she died of pneumonia.

Stead later met a friend of Julia Ames, who told him about her untimely death the previous year. The woman, Miss X, had made a pact with Julia. They had agreed that the first to die would try to make contact with the other. Miss X told Stead that shortly after her death Julia had appeared to her in her room. She now wanted to find a medium who could help her contact Julia again.

In 1892 Stead had discovered that he had the ability for automatic writing, i.e. messages written by a medium under the control of a spirit.

Stead asked Miss X if he could try to reach Julia through automatic writing. The experiment was apparently successful and Miss X was satisfied that Stead had indeed contacted Julia. Stead later published a compilation of the communications which he called "Letters to Julia".

He was fascinated with every aspect of the supernatural. In 1895 whilst attending the Congregational church in Wimbledon he saw a female friend of his among the worshippers. She was also seen by the Clergyman and Deacon. The woman stayed for most of the service and left just before the end.

Stead discovered afterwards, to his surprise, that the woman had been very ill in bed that day and had not actually attended the church.

Tragically, William Stead died on 15th April 1912. He was a passenger on the Titanic which went down when it hit an iceberg. He had had a premonition that he should not travel on the ship, but had ignored it.

Coincidentally, another passenger who also died on that fateful day was an actor, Laurence Irving, who shortly before sailing on the Titanic had performed in 'Typhoon' at Wimbledon Theatre.

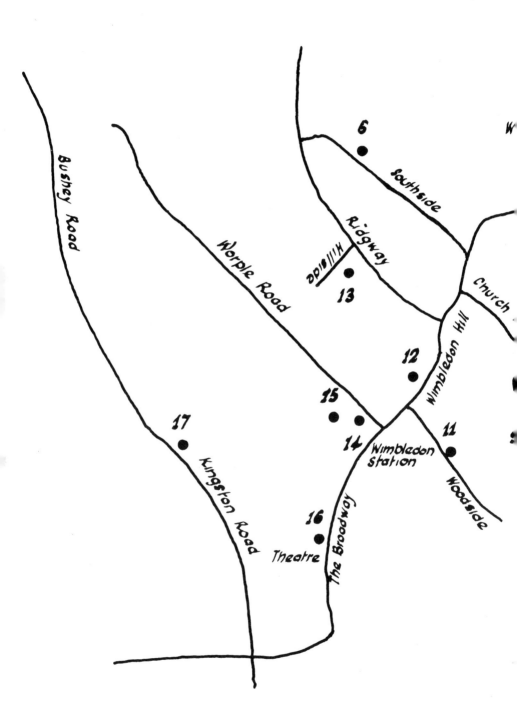

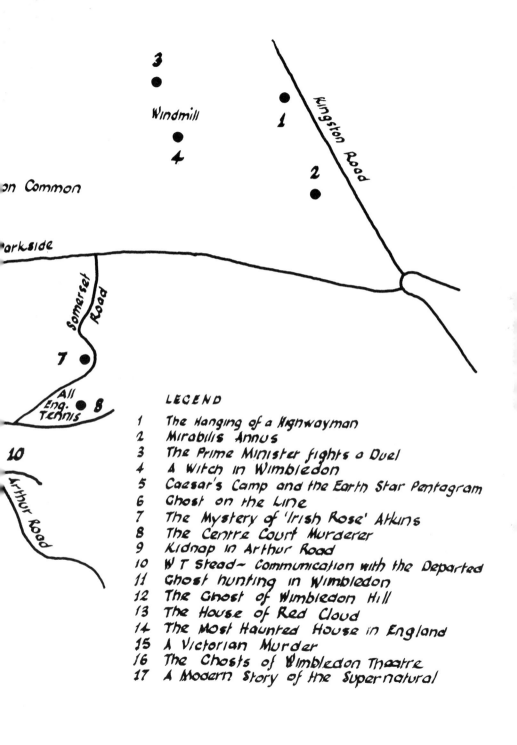

3

Windmill

4

1

2

Kingston Road

on Common

Parkside

Somerset Road

7

All Eng. Tennis

8

10

Arthur Road

THE GHOSTS OF WIMBLEDON THEATRE

There have probably been theatrical ghosts ever since the Greek tragedies but Wimbledon Theatre has not one but two ghosts.

The so-called Grey Lady has been seen many times over the years by usherettes and stagehands as well as by the present Manageress Carol Moon.

In 1980 soon after Carol moved into the flat above the theatre the Grey Lady appeared in her bedroom as a gruesome figure of head and torso only which then left rapidly through the ceiling emitting a raucous cackle.

The Grey Lady has also been seen sitting in the front row of the gallery, in the flytower, where she walked through a closed door, and even coming out of the ladies' toilet!

Her presence has also been felt by more than one psychically aware visitor on a guided tour of the theatre even though they had no previous knowledge of a ghost.

Unfortunately the Grey Lady also has a predilection for practical jokes involving water such as turning on taps in the middle of the night, or even setting off the sprinkler system and flooding the stage. The last time this happened the safety curtain was lowered to prevent the orchestra pit being flooded. But oddly, although the water had indeed got into the pit the safety curtain itself was afterwards found to be dry.

Stranger still, in 1991 when the theatre was being refurbished, a photograph was taken of the front entrance but when the picture had been developed a ghostly figure could be seen at the window of a storeroom which was known to be empty. The photograph is now in the theatre's museum of memorabilia.

The second ghost, that of a gentleman, has appeared in one of the theatre boxes. It has been suggested that it could be the ghost of Mr. Mulholland, the original owner of the theatre who opened it to the public in 1910 and died in 1925.

Both ghosts have been seen over a period of about twenty years but potential theatregoers may be relieved to know that neither has been sighted since 1991.

GHOSTHUNTING IN WIMBLEDON

Apart from his investigations into the hauntings at Borley Rectory mentioned elsewhere in this booklet, the well-known 'psychist' Harry Price also conducted many searches into evidence of hauntings and poltergeists at other locations - including Wimbledon.

In 1935, residents at a house in Woodside reported strange occurrences such as raps, bangs, heavy furniture being moved, footsteps on the stairs, doors opening and closing on their own, and maids being unaccountably locked in rooms. These events occurred even when all the occupants of the house were 'under observation' and when the children of the house were away. (Poltergeist activity is often associated with children).

Accompanied by Professor J.C. Flugel and Dr. C.E.M. Joad, Harry Price went to investigate but found nothing.

The manifestations stopped soon afterwards but then reoccurred briefly five years later in 1940 before abruptly ending for good.

An earlier report of a poltergeist in Wimbledon was that at the home of Colonel G.T. Plunket in July 1909. His wife saw a 'luminous thing' move across the room, hover on the back of a chair, and then explode. Colonel Plunket is said to have heard the explosion but did not see the 'spirit'.

```
* * * * * * * * * * * * * * * * * * * * * * * * * * * * * *
*                                                          *
*   The angel which was recently restored to the roof of   *
*   Wimbledon Theatre was said to have been taken down     *
*   during the second world war due to the fact that German *
*   bombers were using it as a landmark to guage their      *
*   proximity to London.                                    *
*                                                          *
* * * * * * * * * * * * * * * * * * * * * * * * * * * * * *
```

THE PRIME MINISTER FIGHTS A DUEL

It is difficult today to imagine the Prime Minister fighting a duel but this is exactly what happened almost two hundred years ago when William Pitt the Younger drew pistols against a political opponent on Putney Heath.

In the eighteenth century, Wimbledon Common and Putney Heath were notorious as the venues for duels, many of them involving well-known and important figures of the day. They included the Duke of York, the Duke of Wellington and the Earl of Cardigan.

Pitt's opponent was the Whig George Tierney who had criticised Pitt's intention in 1798 to increase the strength of the British navy during the war with France.

Pitt accused Tierney of being opposed to the defence of Britain and was challenged to a duel which was fought on Putney Heath where Pitt lived at Bowling Green House.

Fortunately, both men missed their respective targets with their first pistol shots and their relieved seconds declared that honour had been satisfied on both sides and that the duel was over.

Not so fortunate was Captain Tuckett who was killed in 1840 by the Earl of Cardigan in what was to be one of the last important duels to be fought in England.

It was fought near the windmill in the area which is now the Queensmere pond. The owner of the windmill, who had been given the power to prevent duels being fought at this spot, had been bribed by the Earl to let it go ahead. This bribe, along with the subsequent denials of the Earl that the deceased was in fact Captain Tuckett helped to bring duelling into disrepute and secure its demise.

Perhaps the greatest duel never to be fought on the common was between Prince Louis Napoleon, later Napoleon III of France and his cousin Count Leon in 1840. The police arrived before the duel began and the would-be opponents were taken unceremoniously to Bow Street prison.

IMPORTANT DUELS FOUGHT ON WIMBLEDON COMMON AND PUTNEY HEATH

1652   Lord Chandos v. Col. Compton
1789   Duke of York v. Lt-Col. Lennox
1798   William Pitt the Younger v. GeorgeTierney
1807   Sir Francis Burdett v. John Paull
1809   Lord Castlereagh v. George Canning
1822   Duke of Wellington v. Lord Winchelsea
1839   Marquis of Londonderry v. Henry Gratton
1840   Earl of Cardigan v. Capt. Tuckett

The Prime Minister fights a Duel

THE MOST HAUNTED ROAD IN WIMBLEDON

Is Hillside the most haunted road in Wimbledon? Several residents report strange experiences which cannot easily be explained.

One resident and his wife, who have asked not to be named, have both seen the ghost of a young girl walking in their garden. She is aged about twelve and wears a light close-fitting chemise style garment. She has only been seen twice, once in summer and once on a frosty January night, each time between eleven and twelve. On each occasion she walked towards the house then turned and walked away only to disappear altogether.

There was also apparent poltergeist activity in the same house. The owner witnessed a fork jumping off a dinner table when no-one was anywhere near it.

On another occasion blue inkstains appeared on a ceiling and on a wall even though there was no ink being used in the house. When the owner came to clean off the stains a few days later they had already mysteriously disappeared.

Another man, visiting Hillside, returned to his parked car and found his music cassettes strewn around the interior even though the car was still locked and the alarm active.

At another house in Hillside visitors to an upstairs room found that once inside they could not get out. People outside the door could open it quite easily but those inside were trapped. One night, the resident of the house was alone and became locked in the room. She so strongly felt the presence of a malevolent spirit in there with her that she jumped in terror from the window to escape.

Not far away at a house in Church Road there are also reports of the ghost of a young girl. Dressed in a brown cloak and cowl and wearing a malevolent expression the girl is said to appear immediately prior to unpleasant occurrences at the house such as accidents or deaths.

THE HOUSE OF RED CLOUD

One possible explanation for the intense supernatural activity in Hillside is the fact that from 1934-1941 it was the home of a spiritualist group whose headquarters were known as the House of Red Cloud. The group was run by Estelle Roberts, one of the best known mediums in Britain, whose spirit guide was an American Indian named Red Cloud.

Estelle Roberts had many well-known followers including King George of Greece, Sir Arthur Conan Doyle, and politicians such as Ernest Bevin and George Lansbury.

The House of Red Cloud was opened in October 1934 in the presence of King George of Greece, the Marchioness of Hereford, and distinguished writer Shaw Desmond.

The house was dedicated to 'healing the sick and for demonstrations of Estelle Roberts' psychic gifts'.

Many national spiritualist events were organised from these headquarters, including those organised in conjunction with the Daily Sketch and Sunday Pictorial newspapers.

The house was closed in 1941 when Estelle Roberts was bombed out of her home in Esher and moved to the West Country.

She died in 1970, aged 80.

```
*  *  *  *  *  *  *  *  *  *  *  *  *  *  *  *  *  *  *  *  *  *  *  *  *  *  *  *  *
*                                                                               *
*     The Wimbledon author Captain Marryat once shot a                          *
*     ghost!  Whilst staying at Raynham Hall in Norfolk he                      *
*     encountered the ghost of Dorothy Walpole who was                          *
*     known as the Brown Lady due to the colour of her dress.  *
*     Rather ungallantly he fired his pistol at her, whereupon                  *
*     she disappeared and his bullet lodged in the door                         *
*     behind where she had been standing.                                       *
*                                                                               *
*  *  *  *  *  *  *  *  *  *  *  *  *  *  *  *  *  *  *  *  *  *  *  *  *  *  *  *  *
```

A GHOST ON WIMBLEDON HILL

Not all ghosts stories are confined to ancient buildings and centuries past. A relatively recent ghost is the one which stalked the White House on Wimbledon Hill in the 1980s.

In 1983 the Wimbledon News reported that several of the staff of City Assurance Consultants, the then occupiers of the White House, had seen a ghost on the premises. Even the managing director of the firm, Byron Theo admitted that it had been seen.

The spirit was described as that of an elderly gentleman of benign and friendly nature. He was said to have been immaculately dressed, with grey hair and piercing blue eyes.

One of the firm's directors, Clive Bishop, was startled one night when he was working late and walked downstairs to be confronted by the ghost who turned, looked at him, and then disappeared.

Many people reported having been aware of a ghostly presence in the house, and one room remained inexplicably cold no matter what was done to heat it.

The possible identity of the ghost is uncertain but the house was the home of the Edward-Jones family from the end of the 19th century until the beginning of the Second World War and one theory is that the ghost could have been that of Mr. Edward-Jones who died there at the turn of the century.

MIRABILIS ANNUS

One of the most peculiar episodes in the history of Wimbledon has to be the series of strange events surrounding the death of Nathanial Pace in October 1660.

In 1661 a pamphlet entitled Mirabilis Annus was printed secretly. It was subtitled 'The year of prodigies and wonders, being a faithful and impartial collection of several signs that have been seen in the heavens, in the earth and the waters; together with many remarkable accidents and judgements befalling divers persons, according as they have been testified by very credible hands; all of which have happened within the space of one year last past, and are now made public for a seasonable warning to the people of these three kingdoms speedily to repent and turn to the Lord, whose hand is lifted up amongst us'.

In its eighty-eight pages it presents a list of cataclysmic events such as earthquakes, storms, and unusual incidents, some of which occurred around Wimbledon. For example:

'A bright cloud running to and fro, and dropping fire on Whitehall and Parliament House, seen by boat passengers from Putney'.

'Three suns seen near Kingston on May 14th 1661, from 5 to 7 in the morning, one easterly of the true sun and of blood colour, the other more southerly and half blood, half silver'.

The list also included the death of Nathanial Pace who had disrupted several religious meetings held by the minister of Wimbledon, Mr. Syms; notably one held at Syms' house on October 7th 1660.

The following day, Pace collapsed whilst working on Putney Heath and died a few days later. It is believed that he died from a stroke but what brought this about is not known.

It is thought that the reason his death was mentioned in Mirabilis Annus was because of Syms' links with the millenarium movement which was awaiting the imminent second coming of Christ, and this sudden death indicated the wrath of God being vented towards its critics and opponents.

The Mirabilis Annus pamphlet was regarded as seditious by Charles II's council, and printers and booksellers connected with it were arrested and copies burnt; although it seems that no one was ultimately prosecuted for it.

THE HANGING OF A HIGHWAYMAN

If you go to Tibbet's corner at the northernmost end of Wimbledon Common you will see a commemorative sign depicting a highwayman. His name was not Tibbet as is sometimes assumed, but Jerry Abershawe.

Louis Jeremiah Abershawe (or Avershawe) was said to live in Coombe Wood. He worked Wimbledon Common in the late eighteenth century as it was then a busy route for travellers to Putney and London.

Ever since the establishment of regular coach services in the seventeenth and eighteenth centuries the activities of highwaymen became more and more prevalent. A handful of them even managed to attain a considerable level of infamy. Along with Dick Turpin, Jonathan Wild, and John Nevison, Jerry Abershawe was one of the most notorious.

He and his small gang based themselves at an inn named the Bald-Faced Stag on the Portsmouth Road and were a serious problem locally for several years, waylaying gentry travelling to and from London.

They managed to evade the authorities for almost five years until they were eventually arrested in 1795. In a desperate attempt to avoid capture Jerry Abershawe shot and killed a Bow Street Runner and was sentenced to death.

He was actually hanged on Kennington Common but his body was then hung in chains from a specially erected gallows on what is now known as 'Jerry's Hill' near the Windmill on Wimbledon Common.

This example to others seemed to work as the amount of robberies in the area diminished after this.

The Hanging of a Highwayman

A MODERN STORY OF THE SUPERNATURAL

Although many stories of the supernatural are associated with antiquity such as dusty old castles and haunted churches, this one is connected with that most contemporary of objects, the colour television.

Elsewhere in this booklet we have related the story of how Marconi, the inventor of the radio had an interest in developing a machine that could contact other levels of existence and that since his day others have investigated Electronic Voice Phenomenon or EVP. The following story seems to be another manifestation of this peculiar phenomenon.

On April 28th 1989 Wimbledon resident Treasa Hearty was joining in the party to celebrate her grandson James' birthday. As with most children's parties the family took photographs of the happy day, including one of James standing by the TV, smiling at the camera.

However, when the photograph was developed the TV was seen to have an image on it. This seemed impossible as the TV had been turned off during the birthday party at Treasa's insistence.

Stranger still was the subject of the image - it was a cartoon drawing of John Lennon. In October 1988 an album had been released to tie in with the film 'Imagine', and the logo was a childlike self-portrait of Lennon. This was the image that turned up on the screen.

It is particularly strange for a number of reasons. Even if the TV had been switched on momentarily there was nothing being broadcast that day featuring Lennon and it is unlikely that it would have been an advertisement as the album had been released six months previously. Also, if anyone wanted to fake a picture like this why choose such a jokey subject? Furthermore, the family have not sought to exploit the picture in any way and the authors only found out about the story by chance.

Because of difficulties in adequately reproducing the photograph in this booklet Wimbledon Spiritualist Church in Hartfield Road has kindly agreed to display it for public viewing.

CAESAR'S CAMP AND THE EARTH STAR PENTAGRAM

Most people have probably heard of ley lines and perhaps know that they link ancient and/or sacred sites. However, there may be more to it than this.

In his book Earth Stars, author Chris Street reveals that many ancient sites in and around London also link up to form precise geometric patterns such as pentagrams and hexagrams. These in turn form a vast and intricate network across the capital.

These patterns may be related to ley lines but constitute a separate phenomenon in their own right. Also the main alignments extend far beyond London to other sacred sites around the country.

The south western point of one of the pentagrams is at Caesar's Camp on Wimbledon Common and as you can see on the diagram the other points connect with various ancient sites and churches.

Furthermore, the point of the pentagram at which Caesar's Camp lies is associated in Druidic tradition with Earth (the other four points being fire, water, air, and spirit.). This is appropriate as Caesar's Camp is in fact an earthwork.

According to Chris Street this may be more than mere coincidence as the whole Common area is an important spot on London's energy matrix and probably exerts a beneficial influence over surrounding built-up areas.

It would be fascinating to find that sites such as Caesar's Camp were part of some greater order of planning.

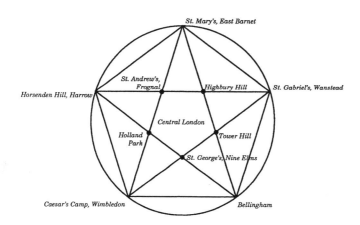

CONCLUSION

We hope that you have enjoyed this look at Mysterious Wimbledon and perhaps learned something new which will make you view the town in a different way.

It is surprising how many strange tales are connected with the area although we are sure there are many others to be told.

If you know any true stories which may fit into possible future editions of this booklet (including not only Wimbledon but also the rest of the borough of Merton) please write to:

ENIGMA PUBLISHING
51 CECIL ROAD
WIMBLEDON
LONDON SW19 1JR

ACKNOWLEDGEMENTS AND THANKS

SPECIAL THANKS TO RICHARD MILWARD FOR ALL HIS HELP AND
ENCOURAGEMENT

BRIAN GOLDSMITH FOR THE WONDERFUL ILLUSTRATIONS

CAROL MOON AND MAURICE WARING OF WIMBLEDON THEATRE

WIMBLEDON SPIRITUALIST CHURCH

TREASA HEARTY

LINDA WILLIAMSON

LYN HAZELL

WIMBLEDON TENNIS MUSEUM

WIMBLEDON MUSEUM & THE WIMBLEDON SOCIETY

WIMBLEDON REFERENCE LIBRARY

LIONEL BEER OF TEMS
(TRAVEL AND EARTH MYSTERIES SOCIETY)

TIM HAIGH (PSYCHIC NEWS)

LEONARD MURPHY, LINDSAY KLATT & CAROLE CHAPMAN

BIBLIOGRAPHY

ALFRED ARBER COOKE	OLD WIMBLEDON
MARTIN FIDO	MURDER GUIDE TO LONDON
RICHARD LAZARUS	THE CASE AGAINST DEATH
ALAN LITTLE	ST LEGER GOOLD
RICHARD MILWARD	HISTORIC WIMBLEDON WIMBLEDON IN THE TIME OF THE CIVIL WAR
HARRY PRICE	POLTERGEISTS OVER ENGLAND
ESTELLE ROBERTS	40 YEARS A MEDIUM
ESTELLE STEAD	W.T. STEAD - MY FATHER
CHRIS STREET	EARTH STARS
ROBERT WOOD	THE WIDOW OF BORLEY